Contents

Introduction

D r. Sebi's diet is drawn from the principles of Dr. Sebi, a native Honduran. Alfredo Darrington Bowman, who's popularly called Dr. Sebi, is a natural healer, herbalist, and intracellular therapist. Dr. Sebi's weight-loss method is quite fascinating and concentrates on consuming natural, alkaline, plant-based foods and herbs, as well as avoiding acidic foods that can cause cellular damage. Dr. Sebi's diet will help followers to prevent mucus build-up and extensively prevent diseases from developing.

If you're interested in starting Dr. Sebi's diet but don't know how to go about it, don't panic! This book will serve as your guide and walk you through the essential basics of the diet.

Also, the book contains recipes that you can try out. The recipes have been expertly assembled and structured in such a way that following them is relatively easy and straightforward.

What the Dr. Sebi Diet Is About

According to Dr. Sebi, diseases are caused by the presence of mucus and acidity in a person's body. He argues that an alkaline environment cannot play host to diseases. Dr. Sebi's program, therefore, involves following strict diets and consuming supplements to achieve detoxification of the body and restore the body to an alkaline, disease-free state.

Simply put, Dr. Sebi's Diet is a vegan diet that forbids any kind of artificial food and hybrid food because the acidity of the foods one eats needs to be reduced, thereby reducing the body's mucus level. Doing these two things reforms the body, making it more alkaline and less prone to accommodate diseases.

Rules of Dr. Sebi's Diet

When you want to follow the alkaline diet, you will need to structure your meals based on the main nutritional guide that has been compiled from over forty years of research. The research period involved finding alkaline, non-hybrid, plant-based foods for consumption.

It is very natural for people to lose weight when their diet pattern is based on Dr. Sebi's alkaline, mucus removing guidelines. This is mainly because they are eating food that does not contain waste, meat, seedless fruits, processed foods, and dairy. In fact, some people choose to practice Dr. Sebi's diet, together with herbs and fasting, to achieve total cleansing, heal some cells in their body, and improve their general well-being. But if you have to combine Dr. Sebi's diet with other procedures, you will need to visit a doctor to make sure you're on the right track.

When you start with the Dr. Sebi diet, you can follow it up for as long as you want if you're able to overcome the obstacles of the first few days. When you start the diet, you will have to deal with the initial challenge of battling sugar cravings. This means you may not be able to eat at restaurants that do not provide a befitting menu for you, and considering that most restaurants serve more fast food and less healthy food, you will need to do most of your cooking at home.

Dr. Sebi's Diet Food Categories

For Dr. Sebi, alkaline foods are the electric foods that allow our cells to be healthy and give off their best performance. For him, food can be grouped into these six groups:

1. Live

2. Raw

3. Dead

4. Hybrid

5. Genetically Modified

6. Drugs

Dr. Sebi's advice is for people to concentrate on eating Live and Raw food while staying away from the rest. He also suggests not eating seedless fruits, weather-resistant crops like corn, and other foods with added minerals or vitamins. It is quite challenging for people to keep to these rules, especially as there are many hybrids and genetically modified vegetables and fruits being sold in grocery stores.

Dr. Sebi recommends that people who desire a healthy life should eat ripe fruits, grains, butter, non-starchy vegetables, and raw nuts. He states that when a person consumes poultry, meat, seafood, yeast-containing products, sugar, iodized salt, alcohol, or fried foods, they negatively affect the body. But when you eat electric foods rather than acidic foods, your body heals faster from the effects of the acid.

Although on the first trial, you may not be comfortable with following a raw diet, you will begin to get used to it when your cells get rid of the toxins and start to cure your disease.

The Benefits of Dr. Sebi's Diet

We already know that reducing the acid level of our food helps to lower mucus in the body, which in turn sets the stage for an alkaline environment that prevents diseases from forming. These are some of the other benefits of following Dr. Sebi's Diet plan:

- **Weight Loss**

Of course, this is just stating the obvious. Weight loss is inevitable when you're eating based on Dr. Sebi's Diet. This is because the diet components are mainly vegetables, fruits, nuts, legumes, and grains. Since you are removing waste, meat, dairy, and processed food, weight loss is simply a natural consequence.

- **Boosts the Immune System**

Diseases and illnesses cause the immune system to become weak. Some people have testified to having a stronger immune system and being cured of some diseases just by following Dr. Sebi's Diet.

- **Lowers Risk of Diseases**

When you consume acidic foods, the mucus membrane of the cells, and the body's inner walls will diminish. This compromises the body system and places you at risk of having diseases. But eating alkaline foods does the opposite and lowers your risk of having diseases as it provides your body cells with the necessary nutrients it needs.

- **Reduces Risk of Stroke and Hypertension**

The National Institute of Health (NIH) states that exercise and weight loss are the first-line therapies for any state of hypertension. But then, after a small study, it has been found that using a plant-based diet to combat hypertension will produce even better results.

In fact, when compared to standard medicine, a plant-based diet does a better job of reducing plaque in the blood vessels, reducing the risk of diabetes, heart disease, and stroke. You can call Dr. Sebi's Diet, a carefully selected plant-based vegan diet.

- **Provides Energy**

Your body's energy levels can be significantly reduced with the intake of meat, white sugar, and dairy. But when you concentrate on consuming plant-based diets, you are increasing your regular energy supply.

- **Heightened Focus**

When you eat, according to Dr. Sebi's teachings, you will find yourself having more clarity, less brain fog, more focus, and less affected when you encounter stress. You don't have to be sick to follow a plant-based diet as it will help improve your life and keep you healthy.

- **Controls the Appetite**

Research has shown that consuming a plant-based meal of peas and beans will make you fuller than eating a meal containing meat.

- **Building the Microbiome**

All the organisms that live in your gut are collectively known as the "microbiome." When you eat more plant-based meals, your microbiome adjusts favorably, and this can prevent diseases.

Permitted Foods in Dr. Sebi's Diet

Dr. Sebi's Diet prohibits all kinds of animal products and promotes vegan eating but on tighter boundaries. For instance, you are not expected to eat seedless fruits, and you can only eat from the grains that are approved by Dr. Sebi's nutritional guide. You must also drink one gallon of natural spring water every day.

These are the foods recommended in the nutritional guide:

- **Fruits:** Apples, bananas, all varieties of berries except cranberries, cantaloupe, currants, cherries, dates, elderberries, figs, seeded grapes, mango, limes, seeded melons, oranges, pawpaw, pears, prickly pears, peaches, plums, prunes, seeded raisins, soursops, soft jelly coconuts, tamarinds.

- **Vegetables:** Avocado, beans (garbanzo), bell peppers, cucumber, chayote, greens (amaranth and dandelion), izote, jale, all lettuce except iceberg, all mushrooms except shiitake, nopales, olives, okra, onions, sea vegetables, cherry, and plum tomato only, squash, tomatillo, greens, watercress, wild arugula, purslane, zucchini.

- **Grains:** Amaranth, Kamut, fonio, quinoa, rye, spelt, tef, wild rice.

- **Natural herbal teas:** Burdock, chamomile, elderberry, fennel, ginger, raspberry, tila.

- **Nuts and seeds:** Brazil nuts, Hemp seeds, raw sesame seeds, raw sesame "tahini" butter, walnuts.

- **Oils:** Avocado oil, coconut oil (not to be cooked), olive oil (not to be cooked), grapeseed oil, hemp seed oil, sesame oil.

- **Seasonings and spices:** Achiote Basil, bay leaf, cayenne, cloves, date sugar, dill, oregano, savory, sweet basil, tarragon, thyme, onion powder, habanero, sage, powdered granulated seaweed, pure agave syrup, pure sea salt.

Foods to Avoid in Dr. Sebi's Diet

- No animal product is permitted, including fish, dairy, and hybrid foods.

- Alcohol is prohibited.

- Wheat is to be avoided and replaced with natural growing grains.

- Canned and seedless food is prohibited.

- Microwaves are not allowed.

Conclusion

Dr. Sebi's is a natural healer, herbalist, and intracellular therapist whose diet has been proven to be of immense health benefit. This diet is based on vegan food items, with no animal products allowed. It works in such a way that it predisposes the body to be in a more alkaline than acidic state. The ideology behind this is that most disease-causing organisms cannot survive in this alkaline state as opposed to an acidic state.

This book did an excellent job of explaining the principle of Dr. Sebi's diet. It also classified food based on Dr. Sebi's rules into live, raw, dead, hybrid, genetically modified, and drugs, with emphasis on consuming only the live and raw foods. The benefits of Dr. Sebi's diet were also covered, while the food items to be consumed and avoided have equally been enumerated.

Whether you are following this diet based on some health-related requirements or general well-being, the result has been proven to be quite remarkable.

Shell Pasta with Mushrooms

Prep Time:	5 minutes	Calories:	220.5
Cook Time:	22 minutes	Fat (g):	9.8
Total Time:	27 minutes	Protein (g):	11.7
Servings:	4	Carbs:	22.1

Ingredients:

Spelt shell pasta	12 oz/340 g
Grapeseed oil	2 tablespoons
White onion, medium, peeled, chopped	1
Cherry tomatoes, chopped	16
Zucchini, chopped	1 cup

Cremini mushrooms, chopped	2 cups
Pure sea salt	1 teaspoon
Dried thyme	1 teaspoon
Raw Sesame Seeds	1 teaspoon

Instructions:

1. Take a large pot, fill it three-fourths full with water, stir in some salt and then place the pot over medium-high heat.

2. Bring the water to a boil, add pasta, and then cook for 10 to 12 minutes or until softened.

3. When done, drain the pasta, reserve ¼ cup of the pasta water, and set aside until required.

4. Take a large skillet pan, add oil to it, place it over medium heat and let it heat until hot.

5. Add chopped onion, zucchini, mushrooms, and tomatoes, and then cook for 5 minutes until vegetables turn tender.

6. Season the vegetables with salt, raw sesame seeds, and thyme, and then cook for 1 minute.

7. Add pasta, pour in reserved pasta water, toss until mixed, and then cook for 2 minutes until hot.

8. Serve straight away.

Spaghetti with Zucchini

Prep Time:	5 minutes	Calories:	248
Cook Time:	40 minutes	Fat (g):	7
Total Time:	45 minutes	Protein (g):	8
Servings:	2	Carbs:	38

Ingredients:

Zucchini, medium, sliced into rounds	1
Pure sea salt	To taste
Dried thyme	½ teaspoon
Grapeseed oil	2 tbsp and more as needed
Spelt spaghetti	8 oz/226 g

Instructions:

1. Switch on the oven, then set it to 350 degrees F (177°C) and let it preheat.

2. Meanwhile, take two baking sheets, line them with parchment paper, and then brush with oil.

3. Spread the zucchini slices on the baking sheet in a single layer, brush with more oil and then sprinkle with salt.

4. Place the baking sheets into the oven and then bake for 30 to 40 minutes until zucchini slices turn golden brown and tender, turning halfway.

5. While zucchini bakes, cook the spaghetti, and for this, take a large pot, fill it three-fourths full with water, stir in some salt and then place the pot over medium-high heat.

6. Bring the water to boil, add pasta, and then cook for 10 to 12 minutes or until softened.

7. When done, drain the spaghetti, return it to the pot, and then set aside until required.

8. When zucchini slices have baked, add them to the pot containing spaghetti, and then drizzle with oil.

9. Season spaghetti with salt and thyme, toss until coated, and then serve.

Pasta with Mushroom and Plum Tomatoes

Prep Time:	5 minutes	Calories:	433.2
Cook Time:	25 minutes	Fat (g):	9
Total Time:	30 minutes	Protein (g):	24.3
Servings:	4	Carbs:	53.4

Ingredients:

Spelt linguine noodles	16 oz/453 g
White onion, medium, peeled, chopped	1
Cremini mushrooms, sliced	6 oz/170 g
Plum tomatoes, cut in half	4 oz/113 g

Dried oregano	¼ teaspoon
Basil leaves	¼ cup
Pure sea salt	¾ teaspoon
Grapeseed oil	1 tablespoon

Instructions:

1. Cook the spaghetti, and for this, take a large pot, fill it three-fourths full with water, stir in some salt and then place the pot over medium-high heat.

2. Bring the water to boil, add pasta, and then cook for 10 to 12 minutes or until softened.

3. When done, drain the pasta and then reserve ¼ cup of pasta water.

4. Meanwhile, take a large skillet pan, place it over medium-high heat, add oil and let it heat.

5. Add onion and then cook for 3 minutes until onion begins to tender.

6. Add mushrooms and then cook for 3 minutes until beginning to brown.

7. Stir in oregano and salt, and then continue cooking for 3 to 5 minutes.

8. Add noodles, pour in the pasta liquid, toss until coated, add basil leaves and tomatoes and then cook for 2 minutes until hot.

9. Taste to adjust seasoning and then serve.

Fruit and Vegetable Salad

Prep Time:	10 minutes	Calories:	320
Cook Time:	0 minutes	Fat (g):	18
Total Time:	10 minutes	Protein (g):	9
Servings:	2	Carbs:	34

Ingredients:

Strawberries, sliced	¼ cup
Blueberries, fresh	¼ cup
Cherries, fresh	¼ cup
Blackberries, fresh	¼ cup

Raspberries, fresh	¼ cup
Currants, fresh	¼ cup
Arugula, fresh	4 oz/113 g
Medium avocado, peeled, pitted, sliced	½
Grapeseed oil	2 tablespoons
Key lime, juiced	1

Instructions:

1. Take a large bowl and then place all the fruits and vegetables in it, except for the avocado.

2. Drizzle with oil and key lime juice, toss until coated.

3. Make a hole in the middle of the bowl and place the avocado in it.

4. Serve.

Spelt Pancakes

Prep Time:	10 minutes	Calories:	103.4
Cook Time:	30 minutes	Fat (g):	1.6
Total Time:	40 minutes	Protein (g):	6
Servings:	5	Carbs:	17.1

Ingredients:

Spelt flour	1 cup (4.23 oz/120 g)
Pure sea salt	1/8 teaspoon

Pure agave syrup	¼ cup (2 fl oz/59 ml)
Grapeseed oil	4 teaspoons
Springwater	as needed
Strawberries, sliced	½ cup
Blueberries, fresh	½ cup
Raspberries, fresh	½ cup

Instructions:

1. Take a large bowl, place flour in it, add salt, 1 teaspoon of oil, and pure agave syrup, stir until just mix and then slowly whisk in water until smooth batter comes together.

2. Take a large skillet pan, place it over medium heat, add the remaining oil and then let it heat until hot.

3. Scoop the prepared batter into the pan, spread like a pancake, and then cook for 2 to 3 minutes per side until golden brown and cooked.

4. Serve the pancakes with berries.

Avocado and Key Lime Pie

Prep Time:	2 h 10 m	Calories:	175.1
Cook Time:	0 minutes	Fat (g):	14.4
Total Time:	2 h 10 m	Protein (g):	2.4
Servings:	6	Carbs:	8.9

Ingredients:

For the Crust:

Walnuts, chopped	1 cup
Amaranth	1 cup (6.81 oz/193 g)
Medjool dates, pitted	2 ½ cups
Coconut oil	3 tablespoons

For the Filling:

Avocado, large, peeled, pitted	1
Walnuts, chopped	1 cup
Coconut milk, soft-jelly	1 cup (8 fl oz/237 ml)
Spelt flour	2 tablespoons
Coconut oil	2 tablespoons
Agave syrup	¼ cup (2 fl oz/59 ml)
Key lime, juiced	2
Pure sea salt	¼ teaspoon

Instructions:

1. Place 1 cup of walnuts into a food processor, add remaining ingredients for the crust, and then pulse until well combined.

2. Spoon the crust mixture into a 9-inch pie pan and then spread evenly in the bottom.

3. Prepare the filling and for this, place all the ingredients in a food processor and then blend until smooth.

4. Spoon the filling over the prepared crust, smooth the top with a spatula and then let it refrigerate for a minimum of 2 hours until set.

5. Cut it into slices, and then serve.

Raspberry Cheesecake

Prep Time:	4 h 30 m	Calories:	314.2
Cook Time:	0 minutes	Fat (g):	20.6
Total Time:	4 h 30 m	Protein (g):	7.6
Servings:	6	Carbs:	30

Ingredients:

For the Crust:

Walnuts, chopped	1 cup
Medjool dates, pitted	13
Pure sea salt	¼ teaspoon

<u>For the Filling</u>:

Raspberries, fresh	2 cups
Cherries, fresh	½ cups
Brazil Nuts, chopped	1 cup
Key lime, juiced	2
Pure sea salt	¼ teaspoon
Medjool dates, pitted	12
Sea moss gel	3 tablespoons

Instructions:

1. Place walnuts into a food processor, add remaining ingredients for the crust in it and then pulse until well combined.

2. Spoon the crust mixture into a springform pan and then spread evenly in the bottom.

3. Prepare the filling, and for this, place raspberries and cherries into the food processor and then pulse until blended.

4. Add brazil nuts, key lime juice, and salt, and then pulse until well combined.

5. Add dates, pulse until incorporated, add sea moss gel into the food processor, and then pulse until combined.

6. Spoon the filling over the prepared crust, and then smooth the top with a spatula.

7. Let it refrigerate for a minimum of 4 hours until set.

8. When done, remove the sides and bottom of the springform pan, scatter some raspberries on top, cut the cake into slices, and then serve.

Squash Cupcakes

Prep Time:	10 minutes	Calories:	121.1
Cook Time:	30 minutes	Fat (g):	1.2
Total Time:	40 minutes	Protein (g):	2.5
Servings:	6	Carbs:	26

Ingredients:

Chickpea flour	1 cup (3.25 oz/92 g)
Spelt flour	2/3 cup (2.82 oz/80 g)
Springwater	¾ cup (6 fl oz/178 ml)
Agave syrup	6 tablespoons

Grapeseed oil	2 tablespoons
Pure sea salt	1/8 teaspoon
Sea moss gel	1 ½ teaspoons
Key lime, juiced	1
Mashed squash, seedless	1 cup

Instructions:

1. Switch on the oven, then set it to 365 degrees F (185°C) and let it preheat.

2. Meanwhile, take a large bowl, place chickpea flour and spelt flour in it, add agave syrup, oil, salt, sea moss gel, and lime juice and then stir until just mixed.

3. Whisk in the water until smooth batter comes together and then fold in mashed squash until combined.

4. Take a six-cup muffin tray, grease it with oil, divide the prepared batter evenly among the cups and then bake for 30 minutes until firm and the top turn golden brown.

5. When done, let the muffins cool for 15 minutes and then serve.

Berries Ice Cream

Prep Time:	2 h 55 m	Calories:	204
Cook Time:	0 minutes	Fat (g):	14.5
Total Time:	2 h 55 m	Protein (g):	2
Servings:	4	Carbs:	18

Ingredients:

Soft-jelly coconut milk	26 fl oz/769 ml
Frozen raspberries, chopped	1/3 cup
Strawberries	½ cup
Agave syrup	¾ cup (6 fl oz/178 ml)
Pure sea salt	¼ teaspoon

Instructions:

1. Pour the milk into the blender, add salt, agave syrup, and then whisk until blended.

2. Add strawberries, blend until just mixed, tip the mixture into a freeze-proof bowl, cover with its lid and then place it into the freezer for 45 minutes.

3. Then stir the ice cream, fold in raspberries and then continue freezing it for 1 hour.

4. After 1 hour, stir the ice cream and then continue freezing it for another 1 hour.

5. Scoop the ice cream into the bowls and then serve.

Avocado, Mushrooms, and Cherry Tomato Salad

Prep Time:	10 minutes	Calories:	161.2
Cook Time:	10 minutes	Fat (g):	12.3
Total Time:	20 minutes	Protein (g):	1.4
Servings:	2	Carbs:	8.9

Ingredients:

Button mushrooms, halved	3 oz/85 g
Grapeseed oil	1 tablespoon
Cherry tomatoes	1 cups
Large avocado, peeled, pitted, sliced	1

Arugula, fresh	3 oz/85 g
Turnip greens	½ cup
Lime juice	1 tablespoon
Pure sea salt	1 teaspoon
Sesame seeds	1 teaspoon

Instructions:

1. Take a large bowl, place the mushrooms halves in it, drizzle with 1 tablespoon of oil, season with ½ teaspoon of salt and then toss until coated.

2. Take a large grill pan, place it over medium-high heat and let it heat.

3. Spread the mushrooms on the pan, cook for 3 to 4 minutes per side until mushrooms turn slightly charred, and then transfer into a large bowl.

4. Add tomatoes, avocado slices, and arugula, sprinkle with the remaining salt, drizzle with 1 tablespoon of lime juice and then toss until coated.

5. Take a large plate, spread turnip greens on it, and then top with mushroom salad.

6. Serve.

Ginger Tea

Prep Time:	5 minutes	Calories:	5
Cook Time:	10 minutes	Fat (g):	0.04
Total Time:	15 minutes	Protein (g):	0.07
Servings:	2	Carbs:	1.2

Ingredients:

Ginger slices	4
Springwater	2 cups (16 fl oz/474 ml)
Chamomile	2 teaspoons

Instructions:

1. Take a medium saucepan, place it over high heat, pour in water, and then add chamomile and ginger slices.

2. Bring the mixture to a simmer, switch heat to medium level and then simmer for 5 minutes.

3. When done, remove the pan from heat, pour the tea among four cups through a mesh sieve and then serve.

Cherries Muffins

Prep Time:	10 minutes	Calories:	210
Cook Time:	30 minutes	Fat (g):	9
Total Time:	40 minutes	Protein (g):	4
Servings:	6	Carbs:	35

Ingredients:

Chickpea flour	1 cup (3.25 oz/92 g)
Spelt flour	2/3 cup (2.82 oz/80 g)
Springwater	¾ cup (6 fl oz/178 ml)
Agave syrup	6 tablespoons

Grapeseed oil	2 tablespoons
Pure sea salt	1/8 teaspoon
Sea moss gel	1 ½ teaspoons
Key lime, juiced	1
Cherries, fresh	½ cup

Instructions:

1. Switch on the oven, then set it to 365 degrees F (185°C) and let it preheat.

2. Meanwhile, take a large bowl, place chickpea flour and spelt flour in it, add agave syrup, oil, salt, sea moss gel, and lime juice, and stir until just mixed.

3. Whisk in the water until smooth batter comes together and then fold in cherries until combined.

4. Take a six-cup muffin tray, grease it with oil, divide the prepared batter evenly among the cups and then bake for 30 minutes until firm and the top turn golden brown.

5. When done, let the muffins cool for 15 minutes and then serve.

Spaghetti with Pesto Sauce and Tomatoes

Prep Time:	10 minutes	Calories:	167.1
Cook Time:	15 minutes	Fat (g):	7.3
Total Time:	25 minutes	Protein (g):	5.6
Servings:	4	Carbs:	20.2

Ingredients:

Spelt spaghetti	12 oz/340 g
Cherry tomatoes, halved	1 cup
Pure sea salt	1/3 teaspoon

For the Pesto:

Basil leaves	1 cup
Walnuts, chopped	1/3 cup
Olive oil	¼ cup (2 fl oz/59 ml)
Pure sea salt	1/3 teaspoon

Instructions:

1. Cook the spaghetti, and for this, take a large pot, fill it three-fourths full with water, stir in some salt and then place the pot over medium-high heat.

2. Bring the water to boil, add pasta, and then cook for 10 to 12 minutes or until softened.

3. Meanwhile, take a large skillet pan, place it over medium-high heat, add oil and let it heat.

4. Add tomatoes and then cook for 3 minutes until tomatoes begin to tender.

5. Then, prepare the pesto and for this, place all of its ingredients in a food processor and then pulse until well blended.

6. When done, drain the pasta, transfer it to a large bowl, and then pour in ½ cup of cooking liquid.

7. Add prepared pesto, toss until coated, add cherry tomatoes and salt and then toss until well combined.

8. Serve straight away.

Apple Pancakes

Prep Time:	10 minutes	Calories:	105.4
Cook Time:	30 minutes	Fat (g):	2
Total Time:	40 minutes	Protein (g):	3.6
Servings:	6	Carbs:	12.6

Ingredients:

For the Pancakes:

Spelt flour	1 cup (4.23 oz/120 g)
Pure sea salt	1/8 teaspoon
Agave syrup	¼ cup (2 fl oz/59 ml)

Grapeseed oil	4 teaspoons
Springwater	as needed
For the Apple Topping:	
Apples, peeled, cored, diced	2
Date sugar	2 tablespoons
Agave syrup	1/3 cup (2.7 fl oz/79 ml)

Instructions:

1. Take a large bowl, place flour in it, add salt, 1 teaspoon of oil, and agave syrup, stir until just mix, and then slowly whisk in water until smooth batter comes together.

2. Take a large skillet pan, place it over medium heat, add the remaining oil and then let it heat until hot.

3. Scoop the prepared batter into the pan, spread like a pancake, and then cook for 2 to 3 minutes per side until golden brown and cooked.

4. When the pancakes have cooked, prepare the apple topping and for this, take a medium saucepan and place it over medium heat.

5. Add apples and date sugar, stir until mixed, and then cook for 3 to 5 minutes until apples have turned very tender.

6. Add agave syrup, stir until well combined, cook for 1 minute and then remove the pan from heat.

7. Spoon the apple topping over the pancakes and then serve.

Tomato Soup

Prep Time:	10 minutes	Calories:	150
Cook Time:	55 minutes	Fat (g):	10
Total Time:	1 h 5 m	Protein (g):	2
Servings:	4	Carbs:	14

Ingredients:

Cherry tomatoes	26
Medium red bell pepper, cored, sliced	1
Medium yellow bell pepper, cored, sliced	1
Pure sea salt	1 ¼ teaspoons
Cayenne pepper	½ teaspoon
Dried oregano	2 teaspoons

Agave syrup	1 teaspoon
Grapeseed oil	1 tsp and 1 tbsp
Large white onion, peeled, chopped	1
Basil leaves, fresh, chopped	½ cup
Dried thyme	1 teaspoon
Springwater	1 cup (8 fl oz/237 ml)

Instructions:

1. Switch on the oven, then set it to 400 degrees F (204°C) and let it preheat.

2. Take a large baking sheet, line it with foil, arrange the tomatoes in it, make a cut in the form of X on each tomato and then add bell pepper slices.

3. Sprinkle 1 teaspoon of salt, cayenne pepper, and 1 teaspoon of oregano over the tomatoes, drizzle with agave syrup and 1 teaspoon of oil and then toss and turn the tomatoes and bell peppers until coated.

4. Place the prepared baking sheet into the oven and then roast the vegetables for 45 minutes until very tender.

5. Then, take a large pot, place it over medium heat, add the remaining oil, and let it heat.

6. Add onion and ¼ cup basil, stir until mixed and then cook for 3 to 4 minutes until onions begin to soften.

7. Add roasted vegetables with their liquid into the pot, sprinkle with thyme, the remaining sea salt, and 1 teaspoon of oregano, and then pour in water.

8. Puree the mixture using a stick blender until smooth soup comes together, and then bring it to a simmer.

9. Add remaining basil, continue cooking the soup for 3 to 5 minutes until soup has thickened to the desired level.

10. Remove pot from heat, ladle soup into bowls and then serve.

Mango Pancakes

Prep Time:	10 minutes	Calories:	147
Cook Time:	15 minutes	Fat (g):	2
Total Time:	25 minutes	Protein (g):	5
Servings:	4	Carbs:	33

Ingredients:

Spelt flour	1 cup (4.23 oz/120 g)
Mango, pureed	½ cup
Pure sea salt	1/8 teaspoon
Pure agave syrup	¼ cup (2 fl oz/59 ml)

| Grapeseed oil | 4 teaspoons |
| Springwater | as needed |

Instructions:

1. Take a large bowl, place flour in it, add salt, 1 teaspoon of oil, agave syrup, mango puree, stir until just mix, and then slowly whisk in water until smooth batter comes together.

2. Take a large skillet pan, place it over medium heat, add the remaining oil and then let it heat until hot.

3. Scoop the prepared batter into the pan, spread like a pancake, and then cook for 2 minutes per side until golden brown and cooked.

4. Serve.

Avocado, Tomato, and Olive Salad

Prep Time:	5 minutes	Calories:	466.2
Cook Time:	0 minutes	Fat (g):	32
Total Time:	5 minutes	Protein (g):	8.4
Servings:	1	Carbs:	23.2

Ingredients:

Medium avocado, peeled, pitted, sliced	1
Black olives, sliced	5
Cherry tomatoes, halved	4
Key limes, juiced	1

Grapeseed oil	2 tablespoons
Pure sea salt	2/3 teaspoon
Lettuce leaves	7

Instructions:

1. Take a large salad bowl and place lettuce leaves on the bottom, then place avocado and tomatoes over the leaves. Add olives to the center of the salad.

2. Drizzle lime juice and oil over the vegetables, sprinkle with salt, and then let it sit for 3 minutes.

3. Serve straight away.

Roasted Bell Pepper Salad

Prep Time:	20 minutes	Calories:	79
Cook Time:	20 minutes	Fat (g):	3
Total Time:	40 minutes	Protein (g):	1
Servings:	2	Carbs:	14

Ingredients:

Medium red bell pepper	2
Medium yellow bell pepper	2
Kalamata olives, pitted	½ cup
Pure sea salt	¾ teaspoon

Dried oregano	½ teaspoon
Grapeseed oil	2 tablespoons
Chopped basil	2 tablespoons

Instructions:

1. Switch on the oven, then set it to 400 degrees F (204°C) and let it preheat.

2. Meanwhile, take a large baking sheet, line it with foil, and then place bell peppers on it.

3. Brush the oil over the bell pepper and then bake for 20 minutes until roasted and begin to char.

4. When done, transfer the bell pepper into a large bowl, cover with a plastic wrap and let the pepper rest for 10 to 15 minutes or until lukewarm.

5. Then remove the stem from each bell pepper, cut into ¾-inch pieces and return them into the bowl.

6. Add remaining ingredients, toss until well mixed and then serve.

Zucchini Spaghetti with Basil Pesto

Prep Time:	10 minutes	Calories:	165.8
Cook Time:	0 minutes	Fat (g):	9.7
Total Time:	10 minutes	Protein (g):	6.5
Servings:	2	Carbs:	14.2

Ingredients:

Zucchini, large, spiralized into noodles	2
Cherry tomatoes, halved	½ cup
For the Pesto:	
Basil leaves, fresh	½ cup

Walnuts	1 tablespoon
Grapeseed oil	1 tablespoon
Key lime, juiced	½
Pure sea salt	1/3 teaspoon

Instructions:

1. Prepare the zucchini noodles and for this, spiralized them by using a vegetable peeler or a spiralizer and then place it in a large bowl.

2. Prepare the pesto and for this, place all of its ingredients in a food processor and then pulse until well blended.

3. Tip the pesto into the zucchini bowls, toss until coated, add cherry tomatoes and then toss until combined.

4. Serve straight away.

Apple and Currants Muffins

Prep Time:	10 minutes	Calories:	180
Cook Time:	30 minutes	Fat (g):	6
Total Time:	40 minutes	Protein (g):	4
Servings:	6	Carbs:	32

Ingredients:

Chickpea flour	1 cup (3.25 oz/92 g)
Spelt flour	2/3 cup (2.82 oz/80 g)
Springwater	¾ cup (6 fl oz/178 ml)
Agave syrup	6 tablespoons

Grapeseed oil	2 tablespoons
Pure sea salt	1/8 teaspoon
Sea moss gel	1 ½ teaspoons
Currants, fresh	½ cup
Apple, cored, chopped	½ cup

Instructions:

1. Switch on the oven, then set it to 365 degrees F (185°C) and let it preheat.

2. Meanwhile, take a large bowl, place chickpea flour and spelt flour in it, add agave syrup, oil, salt, sea moss gel, and stir until just mixed.

3. Whisk in the water until smooth batter comes together, and then fold in currants and apple until combined.

4. Take a six-cup muffin tray, grease it with oil, divide the prepared batter evenly among the cups and then bake for 30 minutes until firm and the top turn golden brown.

5. When done, let the muffins cool for 15 minutes and then serve.

Blueberry Cheesecake

Prep Time:	4 h 30 m	Calories:	351
Cook Time:	0 minutes	Fat (g):	22
Total Time:	4 h 30 m	Protein (g):	1
Servings:	6	Carbs:	33

Ingredients:

For the Crust:

Walnuts, chopped   1 cup

Medjool dates, pitted   13

Pure sea salt   ¼ teaspoon

<u>For the Filling</u>:

Blueberries, fresh	2 ½ cups
Walnuts, chopped	1 cup
Pure sea salt	¼ teaspoon
Medjool dates, pitted	12
Sea moss gel	3 tablespoons

<u>For the Topping</u>:

Blueberries, fresh	1 cup

Instructions:

1. Place 1 cup of walnuts into a food processor, add remaining ingredients for the crust in it and then pulse until well combined.

2. Spoon the crust mixture into a springform pan and then spread evenly in the bottom and along the sides.

3. Prepare the filling, and for this, place blueberries into the food processor and then pulse until blended.

4. Add walnuts and salt, and then pulse until well combined.

5. Add dates, pulse until incorporated, add sea moss gel into the food processor, and then pulse until combined.

6. Spoon the filling over the prepared crust, and then smooth the top with a spatula.

7. Let it refrigerate for a minimum of 4 hours until set.

8. When done, remove the sides and bottom of the springform pan, scatter some blueberries on top, cut the cake into slices, and then serve.

Rice Stuffed Bell Peppers

Prep Time:	15 minutes	Calories:	160.6
Cook Time:	1 h 25 m	Fat (g):	2.7
Total Time:	1 h 40 m	Protein (g):	8.8
Servings:	6	Carbs:	29.9

Ingredients:

Medium bell pepper	6
Wild rice	1 cup
Grapeseed oil	1 ½ tablespoons
Medium white onion, peeled, chopped	1
Orange juice	¼ cup (2 fl oz/59 ml)

Pure sea salt	½ teaspoon
Ground cloves	¼ teaspoon
Chopped walnuts	¼ cup
Springwater	2 ½ cups (20 fl oz/592 ml)

Instructions:

1. Cook the rice, and for this, take a small pot, place it over medium heat, add rice and water and then bring it to a slow boil.

2. Then switch heat to the low level and simmer rice for 25 to 35 minutes until rice turns tender and has absorbed all the cooking liquid.

3. Switch on the oven, then set it to 375 degrees F (190°C), and let it preheat.

4. Then take a medium skillet pan, place it over medium heat, add oil and let it heat.

5. Add onion, cook for 4 to 5 minutes until onion turn golden brown, and then add cooked rice.

6. Add salt and cloves, pour in the orange juice, switch heat to the low level, cook for 4 to 5 minutes until done and then stir in walnuts.

7. Prepare the pepper, and for this, cut the stem about ½-inch down, and then cut a thin sliver from the bottom of each pepper.

8. Take a roasting pan, line it with a parchment sheet, arrange the peppers in it, and then stuff with the cooked rice mixture.

9. Cover the top of stuffed peppers with stems, cover the roasting pan with foil and then bake for 30 minutes until peppers turn tender.

10. Uncover the roasting pan and then continue baking the peppers for 10 minutes or more until golden spots begin to appear on them.

11. Serve straight away.

Chickpea and Avocado Salad

Prep Time:	5 minutes	Calories:	290.5
Cook Time:	0 minutes	Fat (g):	15.6
Total Time:	5 minutes	Protein (g):	7.6
Servings:	4	Carbs:	32.8

Ingredients:

Chickpeas, cooked	2 cups
Arugula	2 cups
Medium avocado, peeled, pitted, sliced	2
Pure sea salt	1 teaspoon

Key lime juice, juiced	2
Grapeseed oil	2 tablespoons

Instructions:

1. Take a large bowl, place chickpeas in it, and then add arugula and avocado.

2. Sprinkle with salt, drizzle with lime juice and grapeseed oil and then toss until mixed.

3. Serve straight away.

Pancakes with Strawberries

Prep Time:	10 minutes	Calories:	171
Cook Time:	25 minutes	Fat (g):	4
Total Time:	35 minutes	Protein (g):	5.7
Servings:	4	Carbs:	28

Ingredients:

Spelt flour	1 cup (4.23 oz/ 120g)
Strawberries, fresh, chopped	½ cup
Pure sea salt	1/8 teaspoon
Pure agave syrup	¼ cup (2 fl oz/59 ml)

Grapeseed oil	4 teaspoons
Springwater	as needed
Chopped walnuts	¼ cup

Instructions:

1. Take a large bowl, place flour in it, add salt, 1 teaspoon of oil, and agave syrup, and then stir until just mix.

2. Slowly whisk in water until smooth batter comes together.

3. Take a large skillet pan, place it over medium heat, add the remaining oil and then let it heat until hot.

4. Scoop the prepared batter into the pan, spread like a pancake, and then cook for 2 to 3 minutes per side until golden brown and cooked.

5. Sprinkle walnuts over the pancakes and serve with strawberries.

Citrus Salad

Prep Time:	5 minutes	Calories:	217
Cook Time:	0 minutes	Fat (g):	20.6
Total Time:	5 minutes	Protein (g):	1
Servings:	4	Carbs:	8.7

Ingredients:

Lettuce, cut into bite-size pieces	4 cups
Seville orange, peeled, sliced	4
Walnuts, chopped	1 cup
Agave syrup	1 tablespoon

| Grapeseed oil | 2 tablespoons |
| Lime juice | 2 tablespoons |

Instructions:

1. Take a large salad bowl, place lettuce in it, and then add orange slices.

2. Take a small bowl, place agave syrup in it, add oil and lime juice, and whisk until combined.

3. Drizzle the agave syrup over the lettuce and oranges, toss until coated, and then sprinkle walnuts on top.

4. Serve straight away.

Warm Mushroom and Arugula Salad

Prep Time:	5 minutes	Calories:	190
Cook Time:	10 minutes	Fat (g):	3
Total Time:	15 minutes	Protein (g):	11
Servings:	4	Carbs:	12

Ingredients:

Button mushrooms, sliced	3 cups
Arugula, fresh	5 oz/142 g
Grapeseed oil	1 tablespoon
Sesame seeds	1 teaspoon
Pure sea salt	1 teaspoon

Instructions:

1. Take a large skillet pan, place it over medium heat, add oil, and let it heat.

2. Add sliced mushrooms, cook for 8 to 10 minutes until tender, and then season with salt.

3. Add arugula, toss until mixed, and then divide mushrooms and arugula evenly among four plates.

4. Sprinkle sesame seeds over the mushroom and arugula salad and then serve.

Spicy Okra

Prep Time:	5 minutes	Calories:	158
Cook Time:	12 minutes	Fat (g):	9
Total Time:	17 minutes	Protein (g):	3.7
Servings:	2	Carbs:	17

Ingredients:

Okra, fresh	12 oz/340 g
Grapeseed oil	3 tablespoons
Cloves	½ teaspoon
Cayenne powder	¼ teaspoon
Pure sea salt	¼ teaspoon

Instructions:

1. Prepare okra, and for this, cut into halves and then spread onto a paper towel in a single layer.

2. Take a medium skillet pan, place it over medium-high heat, add 2 table-spoons of oil and let it heat until hot.

3. Add okra, salt, cayenne powder and the remaining oil and then stir until combined.

4. Cook the okra for 10 to 12 minutes until okra turns crisp, and then serve.

Grilled Vegetable Salad

Prep Time:	10 minutes	Calories:	130.5
Cook Time:	10 minutes	Fat (g):	5.4
Total Time:	20 minutes	Protein (g):	2.8
Servings:	4	Carbs:	19.7

Ingredients:

Large zucchini	2
Large red bell pepper	2
Large yellow bell pepper	2
Grapeseed oil	2 tablespoons

| Pure sea salt | 2 teaspoons |
| Dried oregano | 1 teaspoon |

Instructions:

1. Prepare the vegetables, and for this, cut zucchini into round slices and then cut bell peppers into bite-size pieces.

2. Take a large bowl, place zucchini slices and bell pepper pieces in it, drizzle with oil, add salt and oregano and then toss until well coated.

3. Take a grill pan, place it over medium-high heat and then let it heat until hot.

4. Spread the vegetables in a single layer onto the grill pan, cook for 3 to 4 minutes per side until thoroughly cooked and developed grill marks, and then transfer vegetables to a plate.

5. Repeat with the remaining vegetable slices and then serve.

Blueberry and Banana Muffins

Prep Time:	10 minutes	Calories:	194
Cook Time:	30 minutes	Fat (g):	5.8
Total Time:	40 minutes	Protein (g):	2.6
Servings:	6	Carbs:	34.1

Ingredients:

Chickpea flour	1 cup (3.25 oz/92 g)
Spelt flour	2/3 cup (2.82 oz/80 g)
Springwater	¾ cup (6 fl oz/178 ml)
Agave syrup	6 tablespoons

Grapeseed oil	2 tablespoons
Pure sea salt	1/8 teaspoon
Burro banana, peeled, mashed	3
Sea moss gel	1 ½ teaspoons
Blueberries, fresh	2/3 cup

Instructions:

1. Switch on the oven, then set it to 365 degrees F (185°C) and let it preheat.

2. Meanwhile, take a large bowl, place chickpea flour and spelt flour in it, add agave syrup, oil, salt, sea moss gel, and then stir until just mixed.

3. Add mashed bananas, whisk in water until smooth batter comes together, and fold in berries until combined.

4. Take a six-cup muffin tray, grease it with oil, divide the prepared batter evenly among the cups and then bake for 30 minutes until firm and the top turn golden brown.

5. When done, let the muffins cool for 15 minutes and then serve.

Grilled Zucchini Salad

Prep Time:	10 minutes	Calories:	84
Cook Time:	10 minutes	Fat (g):	5.4
Total Time:	20 minutes	Protein (g):	2.6
Servings:	4	Carbs:	6.1

Ingredients:

Large zucchini	4
Grapeseed oil	4 tablespoons
Pure sea salt	2 teaspoons
Dried thyme	1 teaspoon
Arugula, fresh	5 oz/142 g

Instructions:

1. Prepare the zucchini and for this, cut it into thin lengthwise slices and then place it in a dish.

2. Take a grill pan, place it over medium-high heat and then let it heat until hot.

3. Working on one zucchini slice at a time, brush it with oil, sprinkle with salt and thyme, and then place it onto the grill pan.

4. Cook the zucchini slices for 3 to 4 minutes per side until thoroughly cooked and developed grill marks, and then transfer to a dish.

5. Add arugula to the zucchini slices, toss until just mixed, and then serve.

Avocado Cream Soup

Prep Time:	10 minutes	Calories:	351
Cook Time:	12 minutes	Fat (g):	31.5
Total Time:	22 minutes	Protein (g):	3.3
Servings:	4	Carbs:	9.4

Ingredients:

Medium avocado, peeled, pitted, chopped	4
Medium white onion, peeled, chopped	½
Grapeseed oil	1 tablespoon
Pure sea salt	1 ½ teaspoons

Springwater	3 cups (24 fl oz/711 ml)
Key lime, juiced	1
Soft jelly coconut milk	1 ½ cups (12 fl oz/355 ml)

Instructions:

1. Take a medium pot, place it over medium heat, add oil, and then let it heat.

2. Add onion, cook for 4 to 5 minutes until the onions turn soft, add avocado, pour in the water and coconut milk, and then stir until mixed.

3. Bring the soup to a simmer and then puree the mixture until smooth soup comes together.

4. Stir in salt and lime juice, bring the soup to a simmer, and then cook for 2 to 3 minutes until it has thickened to the desired level.

5. Ladle the soup into bowls and then serve.

Watercress, Mango and Avocado Salad

Prep Time:	5 minutes	Calories:	304
Cook Time:	0 minutes	Fat (g):	22.6
Total Time:	5 minutes	Protein (g):	3
Servings:	4	Carbs:	27.7

Ingredients:

Watercress, fresh	4 cups
Medium mangoes, peeled, destones, diced	2
Medium avocado, peeled, pitted, diced	2
Agave syrup	1 tablespoon

Instructions:

1. Take a salad bowl, place watercress in it, and then add mangoes and avocado pieces.

2. Drizzle with agave syrup, toss until mixed and then serve.

Spaghetti with Cherry Tomatoes and Basil

Prep Time:	10 minutes	Calories:	323.7
Cook Time:	15 minutes	Fat (g):	10.6
Total Time:	25 minutes	Protein (g):	10.2
Servings:	4	Carbs:	50.1

Ingredients:

Cherry tomatoes, cut in half	2 cups
Pure sea salt	1 teaspoon
Basil leaves, sliced	6
Grapeseed oil	2 teaspoons
Spelt spaghetti	16 oz/453 g

Instructions:

1. Cook the spaghetti, and for this, take a large pot, fill it three-fourths full with water, stir in some salt and then place the pot over medium-high heat.

2. Bring the water to a boil, add pasta, and then cook for 10 to 12 minutes or until softened.

3. Meanwhile, take a large skillet pan, place oil in it and when hot, add tomatoes and sliced basil leaves, cook for 2 minutes, season with salt, stir until mixed and then remove the pan from heat.

4. When done, drain the spaghetti and then reserve ½ cup of the pasta liquid.

5. Add pasta into the tomato mixture, pour in the reserved pasta water, and then toss until combined.

6. Serve.

Arugula and Cherry Tomato Salad

Prep Time:	5 minutes	Calories:	187.3
Cook Time:	0 minutes	Fat (g):	16.9
Total Time:	5 minutes	Protein (g):	1.4
Servings:	1	Carbs:	5.9

Ingredients:

Arugula, fresh	6 oz/170 g
Cherry tomatoes, halved	1 cup
Large avocado, peeled, pitted, sliced	½
Key lime, juiced	½

Instructions:

1. Take a large salad bowl, place arugula in it, add tomatoes and then drizzle with key lime juice.

2. Toss until mixed, top the salad with avocado slices and then serve.

Blueberries Pancakes

Prep Time:	10 minutes	Calories:	195.6
Cook Time:	25 minutes	Fat (g):	8.4
Total Time:	35 minutes	Protein (g):	6.8
Servings:	4	Carbs:	24

Ingredients:

Spelt flour	1 cup (4.23 oz/120 g)
Blueberries, fresh	½ cup
Pure sea salt	1/8 teaspoon
Pure agave syrup	¼ cup (2 fl oz/59 ml)

Grapeseed oil	4 teaspoons
Springwater	as needed

Instructions:

1. Take a large bowl, place flour in it, add salt, 1 teaspoon of oil, and agave syrup, and then stir until just mix.

2. Slowly whisk in water until smooth batter comes together and then fold in berries until just mixed.

3. Take a large skillet pan, place it over medium heat, add the remaining oil and then let it heat until hot.

4. Scoop the prepared batter into the pan, spread like a pancake, and then cook for 2 to 3 minutes per side until golden brown and cooked.

5. Serve straight away.

Cucumber and Tomato Salad

Prep Time:	5 minutes	Calories:	26
Cook Time:	0 minutes	Fat (g):	0
Total Time:	5 minutes	Protein (g):	1
Servings:	4	Carbs:	6

Ingredients:

Cherry tomatoes, halved	3 cups
Medium cucumber, diced	2
Purslane (Verdolaga), fresh	2 cups
Key lime, juiced	2
Pure sea salt	½ teaspoon

Instructions:

1. Take a large bowl, add cherry tomatoes, and then cucumber and purslane.

2. Season with salt, drizzle with lime juice and then toss until mixed.

3. Serve straight away.

Berries and Banana Salad

Prep Time:	5 minutes	Calories:	74
Cook Time:	0 minutes	Fat (g):	0.3
Total Time:	5 minutes	Protein (g):	1.5
Servings:	4	Carbs:	18.1

Ingredients:

Burro banana	4
Strawberries, fresh, diced	2 cups
Blueberries, fresh	2 cups
Agave syrup	4 tablespoons

Instructions:

1. Peel the bananas and then cut them into round slices.

2. Take a salad bowl, place banana slices in it, and then add strawberries and blueberries.

3. Drizzle agave syrup over the fruits, then toss until coated, and serve.

Cherry Ice Cream

Prep Time:	2 h 55 m	Calories:	293
Cook Time:	20 minutes	Fat (g):	21.5
Total Time:	3 h 15 m	Protein (g):	3.3
Servings:	4	Carbs:	26.5

Ingredients:

Cherries, pitted	5 cups
Homemade Soft-jelly coconut cream	19 oz/539 g
Agave syrup	¼ cup (2 fl oz/59 ml)

Instructions:

1. Switch on the oven, then set it to 300 degrees F (149°C) and let it preheat.

2. Meanwhile, take a medium baking sheet and then spread 2 cups of cherries on it in a single layer.

3. Place the cherries into the oven, roast them for 20 minutes and when done, transfer cherries to a plate and let them refrigerate until cooled.

4. While cherries are roasting, place remaining cherries into a blender, add coconut cream and agave syrup and then pulse until smooth.

5. Spoon the blended cherry mixture into a freeze-proof bowl, cover with its lid and then place it into the freezer for 45 minutes.

6. Then stir the ice cream, fold in roasted cherries and then continue freezing it for 1 hour.

7. After 1 hour, stir the ice cream and then continue freezing it for another 1 hour.

8. Scoop the ice cream into the bowls and then serve.

Peach Muffins

Prep Time:	10 minutes	Calories:	135
Cook Time:	30 minutes	Fat (g):	6.9
Total Time:	40 minutes	Protein (g):	3.3
Servings:	6	Carbs:	21.6

Ingredients:

Chickpea flour	1 cup (3.25 oz/92 g)
Spelt flour	2/3 cup (2.82 oz/80 g)
Springwater	¾ cup (6 fl oz/178 ml)

Agave syrup	6 tablespoons
Grapeseed oil	2 tablespoons
Pure sea salt	1/8 teaspoon
Ground cinnamon	1/8 teaspoon
Sea moss gel	1 ½ teaspoons
Peaches, fresh, pitted, chopped	2
Key lime, juiced	1

Instructions:

1. Switch on the oven, then set it to 365 degrees F (185°C) and let it preheat.

2. Meanwhile, take a large bowl, place chickpea flour and spelt flour in it, and then stir until mixed.

3. Add agave syrup, oil, salt, sea moss gel, and lime juice, stir until just mixed, and then whisk in water until smooth batter comes together. Fold in peaches until combined.

4. Take a six-cup muffin tray, grease it with oil, divide the prepared batter evenly among the cups and then bake for 30 minutes until firm and the top turn golden brown.

5. When done, let the muffins cool for 15 minutes and then serve.

Hummus

Prep Time:	5 minutes	Calories:	172
Cook Time:	0 minutes	Fat (g):	4.5
Total Time:	5 minutes	Protein (g):	8.5
Servings:	4	Carbs:	26.1

Ingredients:

Cooked chickpeas	14 oz/397 g
Pure sea salt	½ teaspoon
Basil	½ teaspoon
Oregano	½ teaspoon

Key lime, juiced	1
Sesame seeds	1 tablespoon
Springwater	½ cup (4 fl oz/118 ml)
Grapeseed oil	2 tablespoons

Instructions:

1. Place the chickpeas in a blender, add all the ingredients except for oregano and oil, and then pulse until blended and smooth.

2. Tip the hummus in a medium bowl, sprinkle with oregano, drizzle with oil and then serve.

Quinoa and Amaranth Porridge

Prep Time:	10 minutes	Calories:	218.6
Cook Time:	35 minutes	Fat (g):	6
Total Time:	45 minutes	Protein (g):	8.9
Servings:	4	Carbs:	33.1

Ingredients:

Amaranth, rinsed	½ cup
Quinoa, rinsed	½ cup
Springwater	2 cups (16 fl oz/474 ml)
Soft-jelly coconut milk	½ cup (4 fl oz/118 ml)

Instructions:

1. Take a small pan, place it over medium-high heat, add quinoa and amaranth, pour in water, and then bring to a boil.

2. Switch heat to the low level, simmer for 25 minutes until grains have absorbed all the liquid, stir in milk, and then continue simmering for 10 minutes until porridge turns creamy.

3. Then remove the pan from heat, and let the porridge sit for 5 minutes or until thicken and cool slightly.

4. Divide the porridge evenly among four bowls, serve it with grilled vegetables.

Banana Pancakes

Prep Time:	10 minutes	Calories:	256.6
Cook Time:	30 minutes	Fat (g):	3.6
Total Time:	40 minutes	Protein (g):	9.3
Servings:	5	Carbs:	48.4

Ingredients:

Burro banana, peeled	2
Walnut milk	1 ½ cups (12 fl oz / 355 ml)
Pure agave syrup	1 tablespoon
Grapeseed oil	1 ½ teaspoons

| Teff flour | 1 ½ cups (8.68 oz/246 g) |
| Pure sea salt | ¼ teaspoon |

Instructions:

1. Place bananas in a blender, add agave syrup, ½ teaspoon of oil, and milk, and then pulse until well combined.

2. Take a large bowl, place flour in it, add salt , pour in banana mixture, and then whisk well until smooth batter comes together.

3. Take a large skillet pan, place it over medium heat, add the remaining oil and then let it heat until hot.

4. Scoop the prepared batter into the pan, spread like a pancake, and then cook for 2 to 3 minutes per side until golden brown and cooked.

5. Serve straight away with banana slices.

Spaghetti with Tomato Sauce

Prep Time:	10 minutes	Calories:	271
Cook Time:	1 h 10 m	Fat (g):	4.7
Total Time:	1 h 20 m	Protein (g):	9.4
Servings:	4	Carbs:	49

Ingredients:

For the Tomato Sauce:

Cherry tomatoes	5 cups
Dried oregano	1 tablespoon
Pure sea salt	1 tablespoon
Cayenne pepper	½ teaspoon

Pure Agave Syrup	1 tablespoon
Grapeseed oil	1 tablespoon
Basil	1 tablespoon
Bay leaf	1
For the Spaghetti:	
Spelt spaghetti	16 oz/453 g
Grapeseed oil	2 tablespoons

Instructions:

1. Prepare the tomatoes and for this, peel them and then make a small x-shape cut on both ends of the tomatoes.

2. Take a medium pot, fill it half full with water, place it over medium-high heat and then bring it to a boil.

3. Add tomatoes, boil for 1 minute, then transfer tomatoes to a bowl containing chilled water and let them soak for 30 seconds.

4. Transfer tomatoes into a blender, add remaining ingredients for the sauce except for bay leaf, and then pulse until blended.

5. Pour the sauce into a large pot, place it over medium heat, add bay leaf into the sauce and then simmer for 45 to 60 minutes until thoroughly cooked and thicken.

6. Meanwhile, cook the spaghetti and for this, take a large pot, fill it three-fourths full with water, stir in some salt and then place the pot over medium-high heat.

7. Bring the water to boil, add pasta, and then cook for 10 to 12 minutes or until softened.

8. When done, drain the spaghetti, return it into the pot, drizzle with oil, toss until coated, and then set aside until required.

9. When the sauce has cooked, taste it to adjust seasoning, add spaghetti, and toss it until coated.

10. Cook the spaghetti for 2 minutes until hot and then serve.

Strawberry Cheesecake

Prep Time:	4 h 30 m	Calories:	287.8
Cook Time:	0 minutes	Fat (g):	24.2
Total Time:	4 h 30 m	Protein (g):	3.5
Servings:	6	Carbs:	10.5

Ingredients:

For the Crust:

Walnuts, chopped	1 cup
Medjool dates, pitted	13
Pure sea salt	¼ teaspoon

For the Filling:

Strawberries, fresh	2 cups
Walnuts, chopped	1 cup
Key lime, juiced	2
Pure sea salt	¼ teaspoon
Medjool dates, pitted	12
Sea moss gel	3 tablespoons

Instructions:

1. Place 1 cup of walnuts into a food processor, add remaining ingredients for the crust in it, and then pulse until well combined.

2. Spoon the crust mixture into a springform pan and then spread evenly in the bottom.

3. Prepare the filling, and for this, place strawberries into the food processor and then pulse until blended.

4. Add walnuts, key lime juice, and salt, and then pulse until well combined.

5. Add dates, pulse until incorporated, add sea moss gel into the food processor, and then pulse until combined.

6. Spoon the filling over the prepared crust, and then smooth the top with a spatula.

7. Let it refrigerate for a minimum of 4 hours until set.

8. When done, remove the sides and bottom of the springform pan, cut the cake into slices, and then serve.

Blueberry Muffins

Prep Time:	10 minutes	Calories:	212
Cook Time:	30 minutes	Fat (g):	9
Total Time:	40 minutes	Protein (g):	2.5
Servings:	6	Carbs:	30

Ingredients:

Chickpea flour	1 cup (3.25 oz/92 g)
Spelt flour	2/3 cup (2.82 oz/80 g)
Springwater	¾ cup (6 fl oz/178 ml)
Agave syrup	6 tablespoons

Grapeseed oil	2 tablespoons
Pure sea salt	1/8 teaspoon
Avocado, peeled, cored, mashed	1
Sea moss gel	1 ½ teaspoons
Key lime, juiced	1
Blueberries, fresh	2/3 cup

Instructions:

1. Switch on the oven, then set it to 365 degrees F (185°C) and let it preheat.

2. Meanwhile, take a large bowl, place chickpea flour and spelt flour in it, add agave syrup, oil, salt, sea moss gel, and lime juice and then stir until just mixed.

3. Add mashed avocado, whisk in water until smooth batter comes together, and fold in berries until combined.

4. Take a six-cup muffin tray, grease it with oil, divide the prepared batter evenly among the cups and then bake for 30 minutes until firm and the top turn golden brown.

5. When done, let the muffins cool for 15 minutes and then serve.

Mushrooms Cream Soup

Prep Time:	10 minutes	Calories:	270
Cook Time:	11 minutes	Fat (g):	24
Total Time:	21 minutes	Protein (g):	7
Servings:	4	Carbs:	8

Ingredients:

Button mushrooms, chopped	8 oz / 227 g
Medium white onion, peeled, chopped	½
Grapeseed oil	1 tablespoon
Spelt flour	1 tablespoon

Pure sea salt	1 ½ teaspoons
Springwater	4 cups (32 fl oz/948 ml)
Soft jelly coconut milk	1 ½ cups (12 fl oz/355 ml)

Instructions:

1. Take a medium pot, place it over medium heat, add oil, and then let it heat.

2. Add mushrooms and onion, cook for 5 to 8 minutes until the vegetables turn soft, pour in the water and coconut milk, and then stir until mixed.

3. Whisk in flour and then puree the mixture until smooth soup comes together.

4. Stir in salt, bring the soup to a simmer and then cook for 2 to 3 minutes until it has thickened to the desired level.

5. Ladle the soup into bowls and then serve.

Chinese Cucumber Salad

Prep Time:	15 minutes	Calories:	68
Cook Time:	0 minutes	Fat (g):	1
Total Time:	15 minutes	Protein (g):	1
Servings:	4	Carbs:	13

Ingredients:

Large cucumber	4
Cayenne, cored, chopped	½
Lime juice	1 tablespoon
Grapeseed oil	1 teaspoon

| Pure sea salt | 1/8 teaspoon |
| Sesame seeds | 1 teaspoon |

Instructions:

1. Prepare the cucumber and for this, remove its end, use a vegetable peeler to slice the cucumber lengthwise and then continue slicing by turning it at 90 degrees, stopping at the seedy part.

2. Take a large salad bowl, add cucumber slices and then add chopped cayenne pepper.

3. Take a small bowl, place the lime juice, oil, and salt, stir until combined, and then drizzle over the cucumber slices.

4. Toss until coated, sprinkle with sesame seeds, and then serve.

Peach Ice Cream

Prep Time:	2 h 55 m	Calories:	199
Cook Time:	0 minutes	Fat (g):	12.3
Total Time:	2 h 55 m	Protein (g):	2.1
Servings:	4	Carbs:	23.2

Ingredients:

Soft-jelly coconut milk	12 fl oz/355 ml
Peaches, pitted, sliced	4
Agave syrup	1/3 cup (2.7 fl oz/79 ml)

Instructions:

1. Add peaches into the blender, pour in the milk, add agave syrup and then whisk until blended.

2. Tip the mixture into a freeze-proof bowl, cover with its lid and then place it into the freezer for 45 minutes.

3. Then stir the ice cream, and then continue freezing it for 1 hour.

4. After 1 hour, stir the ice cream and then continue freezing it for another 1 hour.

5. Scoop the ice cream into the bowls and then serve.

Fruit Salad

Prep Time:	5 minutes	Calories:	57
Cook Time:	0 minutes	Fat (g):	0.1
Total Time:	5 minutes	Protein (g):	2.1
Servings:	4	Carbs:	11.8

Ingredients:

Large mangoes, peeled, pitted, diced	1
Strawberries, halved	½ cup
Raspberries, fresh	½ cup
Blackberries, fresh	½ cup

Blueberries, fresh	½ cup
Cherries, fresh	½ cup
Agave syrup	3 tablespoons
Currants, fresh	½ cup

Instructions:

1. Take a large salad bowl, place all ingredients in it.

2. Drizzle agave syrup over the fruits, then toss until coated, and serve.

Raspberry Tea

Prep Time:	5 minutes	Calories:	9.7
Cook Time:	15 minutes	Fat (g):	0
Total Time:	20 minutes	Protein (g):	0.02
Servings:	2	Carbs:	2.5

Ingredients:

Frozen raspberries, thawed	1 cup
Chamomile tea, brewed	2 cups (16 fl oz/474 ml)
Cloves	¼ teaspoon
Lime, sliced	1

Instructions:

1. Take a large saucepan, add raspberries to it, and then mash with a potato masher.

2. Pour in tea, cloves, and lime slices, bring the mixture to a boil, switch heat to medium-low level, and then simmer for 10 minutes.

3. When done, strain the tea into two mugs and then serve.

Printed in Great Britain
by Amazon